Withdrawn

CRYPTS, TOMBS, AND SECRET ROOMS

THE ROMAN CATACOMBS

BY ENZO GEORGE

Gareth Stevens
PUBLISHING

Please visit our website, www.garethstevens.com. For a free color catalog of all our high-quality books, call toll free 1-800-542-2595 or fax 1-877-542-2596.

Cataloging-in-Publication Data
Names: George, Enzo.
Title: The Roman catacombs / Enzo George.
Description: New York : Gareth Stevens Publishing, 2018. | Series: Crypts, tombs, and secret rooms | Includes index.
Identifiers: ISBN 9781538206614 (pbk.) | ISBN 9781538206553 (library bound) | ISBN 9781538206430 (6 pack)
Subjects: LCSH: Rome--Civilization--Juvenile literature. | Rome--History--Juvenile literature. | Rome--Religious life and customs--Juvenile literature. | Catacombs--Italy--Rome.
Classification: LCC DG77.G47 2018 | DDC 937--dc23

Published in 2018 by
Gareth Stevens Publishing
111 East 14th Street, Suite 349
New York, NY 10003

For Brown Bear Books Ltd:
Managing Editor: Tim Cooke
Designer: Lynne Lennon
Editorial Director: Lindsey Lowe
Children's Publisher: Anne O'Daly
Design Manager: Keith Davis
Picture Manager: Sophie Mortimer

Picture credits:
Cover: Getty: De Agostini / G. Dagli Orti
Interior: Art Gallery of South Australia: 28; **Dreamstime:** 37, Rafael Ben-ari 13, Diego Fiore 8, David Ionut 13; **Kerie Kerstetter:** 5; **Kircherian Collection:** 19; **Public Domain:** 20, 26, 30, 34, 40, Dnalor 14, 16, 22, 27, 31, 43, Lalupa 41, Musée national du Moyen-Age, Cluny 10, Rome Cultural Archives 21, Rome History & Cultural Archives/Franciscus Contini 18, Mike Wilson 7; **Shutterstock:** 39, Steven Bostock 11, John Copland 38, Kobby Dagan 25, ESB Projessional 42, David Gilder 36, Morphart Creation 24, 32, moutainpix 9, pointbreak 6, Luis Santos 35; **Thinkstock:** istockphoto 21; **University of Seville:** Antiquities Library 29, 33; **Walters Art Museum:** 23.

All other images Brown Bear Books

Printed in the United States of America
CPSIA compliance information: Batch CS17GS: For further information contact Gareth Stevens, New York, New York at 1-800-542-2595.

CONTENTS

WORDS IN THE GLOSSARY APPEAR IN **BOLD** TYPE
THE FIRST TIME THEY ARE USED IN THE TEXT.

BENEATH

Deep below the busy streets of the Italian capital city of Rome lies a hidden world. A network of passages, rooms, and galleries stretches for over 100 miles (160 km). Almost 2,000 years ago, these tunnels were carved into the rock beneath the city to make tombs, or **catacombs.**

The tombs were used for a few hundred years but were then abandoned. They were forgotten, and their entrances were buried beneath vegetation and debris. The tunnels lay untouched for over 1,000 years before they were accidentally rediscovered in the 1500s. Even today, only part of the vast network of catacombs has been **excavated**. **Archaeologists** are still unsure about the best way to examine these ancient tombs. These experts are still learning the complete story of who built the catacombs and why.

A network of tunnels has been hidden beneath Rome's streets for nearly 2,000 years.

5

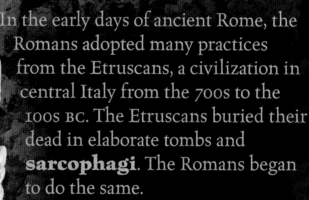

In the early days of ancient Rome, the Romans adopted many practices from the Etruscans, a civilization in central Italy from the 700s to the 100s BC. The Etruscans buried their dead in elaborate tombs and **sarcophagi**. The Romans began to do the same.

From around 250 BC, it became more common for the Romans to dispose of bodies by **cremating** them. They stored the ashes in special containers. Cremation remained common until the first and second centuries AD. Around the first century AD, however, people in Rome also started to bury their dead underground.

This stone urn once held the ashes of a wealthy Roman who had been cremated after his death.

Why they chose to do this is still not really known. At the time, it was illegal to bury the dead anywhere inside Rome itself, so the catacombs were built outside the city walls.

A SPRAWLING NETWORK

Experts think that the first people in Rome to bury their dead underground were probably Jews. They were part of the Jewish **diaspora**, meaning they had moved from their homeland in Palestine to settle elsewhere.

The first catacombs were built under the second and third **milestones** of the Appian Way. The Appian Way was a key highway linking Rome with southern Italy.

The Appian Way milestones were said to be the places where two of the Biblical **apostles**, Peter and Paul, had been buried. This connection once led historians to believe that Christians built the first catacombs. Today, however, experts think that Christians only began to use the catacombs after the Jews had built them.

The ancient Romans did not decorate their tombs or bury objects with the bodies. There is little evidence to help figure out just who was buried where. Many of the underground tombs are still unexcavated. Experts do not even know for certain how many people are buried there. Some estimates suggest that 150,000 bodies were placed in the catacombs from around 25 BC to AD 325.

Emperor Diocletian's persecution of Christians began in 303. Thousands lost their lives throughout the empire.

EARLY CHRISTIANITY

FTER THE DEATH OF JESUS IN THE 30s AD, CHRISTIANITY WAS BANNED
THE ROMAN EMPIRE. CHRISTIANS WERE **PERSECUTED** AND PUNISHED,
FTEN WITH DEATH. UNDER THE EMPEROR DIOCLETIAN IN THE EARLY 300s,
HRISTIANS SUFFERED A PARTICULARLY BRUTAL PERIOD KNOWN AS THE
GREAT PERSECUTION." THE PERSECUTION ENDED WHEN THE EMPEROR
ONSTANTINE **CONVERTED** TO CHRISTIANITY IN 312. ROME THEN TOLERATED

The oldest of the catacombs were said to contain the tomb of Saint Paul.

In the 300s, the population of the area around Rome was likely over 750,000 people. What happened to the bodies of all the other people who died in the city? Archaeologists do not know for certain.

HOW WERE THEY BURIED?

Inside the catacombs, a few corpses were placed in stone coffins in **niches** carved into the walls. Far more bodies were buried without a coffin. They were simply stacked one on top of another. This suggests that the people had been too poor to pay for coffins or **funerary** goods.

WERE THE TOMBS PLANNED?

Archaeologists think that little planning went into the building of the catacombs. The different tunnels spread out in a random way. When an area became full, builders simply burrowed a new passage through the rock to make another tomb. As a result, passages stretch in all different directions. Even today, it is very easy to get lost underground.

OTHER CATACOMBS

THE WORD "CATACOMB" COMES FROM THE LATIN *CATA TUMBAS*, WHICH MEANS "AMONG TOMBS." UNTIL 1836, THE WORD WAS ONLY USED TO DESCRIBE THE CATACOMBS IN ROME. TODAY, THE WORD APPLIES TO ANY UNDERGROUND SYSTEM OF TOMBS. OUTSIDE ROME, THE MOST FAMOUS CATACOMBS ARE IN PARIS, FRANCE. UNLIKE THE ROMAN CATACOMBS, THE PARISIAN CATACOMBS WERE CAREFULLY PLANNED. IN THE 1700s, THE CITY GOVERNMENT DECIDED TO MOVE THE BONES FROM OVERCROWDED GRAVEYARDS TO THE CATACOMBS.

In parts of the Paris Catacombs, the walls are made from the bones and skulls of the dead.

11

Rome lies on a bed of **volcanic** rock called tufa. When tufa is covered with soil it remains soft and easy to quarry. It only hardens when it is exposed to the air. Romans quarried tufa to create magnificent buildings such as the Colosseum.

Centuries after the great buildings of Rome were constructed, Jews, Christians, and other groups who did not follow the Roman religion began to build underground tombs. It was easy for them to dig down beneath the ground.

DIFFERENT CATACOMBS

Experts have found more than 60 catacombs, and they think more are still to be discovered. The Jewish catacombs were among the first to be dug. They tend to be smaller and simpler than Christian catacombs. As far as experts can tell, however, followers of different religions were often buried together.

In the early centuries AD, Jews and Christians usually came from among Rome's poorest groups. Many were slaves.

Few people could afford to buy land, so experts do not know how land was acquired for the catacombs. Evidence suggests some land may have been gifted by rich supporters. However, some experts believe some groups of people may have simply dug into the ground and hoped nobody would notice.

HOW THE CATACOMBS WERE DUG

To construct a catacomb, a narrow staircase was dug down into the tufa. The staircase was usually 23 to 62 feet (7–19 m) deep, but some reached 65 feet (20 m) underground. At the foot of the stairway, a horizontal gallery was dug out. The galleries typically measured around 8 by 3 feet (2 × 1 m). As more burial space was needed, additional galleries were excavated at right angles to the original gallery.

UNDERGROUND BURIALS

HISTORIANS THINK THAT JEWS LIVING IN ROME WERE THE FIRST PEOPLE TO BURY THEIR DEAD UNDERGROUND IN THE CITY. IN THEIR HOMELAND IN PALESTINE, THEY HAD LONG BURIED THEIR DEAD IN TOMBS CUT OUT OF ROCK. AS THE JEWS MOVED AWAY FROM PALESTINE, THEY CONTINUED THEIR CUSTOM OF BURYING THEIR DEAD IN UNDERGROUND TOMBS WHEREVER IT WAS POSSIBLE TO DO SO. EARLY CHRISTIANS AND **PAGANS** LIVING IN ROME ADOPTED THE JEWISH PRACTICE AND BEGAN CONSTRUCTING UNDERGROUND TOMBS.

Jews carved tombs in rocky cliffs at Beit She'arim in what is now Israel from the 100s to the 300s AD.

15

As they dug the galleries, the builders carved niches into the sides to hold the bodies. These niches measured between 47 and 59 inches (120–150 cm) in length and between 16 and 24 inches (40–60 cm) in height. The bodies placed inside these niches were those of wealthier Romans. They were wrapped in linen and placed inside a stone sarcophagus. The niche was then sealed with a stone slab marked with the name, age, and date of death of the dead person. Today, most of the **inscriptions** have worn away over time.

When people ran out of space, they dug deeper. Builders might lower the floor of an existing gallery to create more space. They might also simply dig a whole new level beneath the existing one. Some catacombs have four stories.

COLLAPSING CITY

THE ANCIENT ROMANS DUG OUT TUFA FROM THE GROUND TO BUILD THEIR CITY. THAT LEFT A SERIES OF NARROW UNDERGROUND PASSAGEWAYS WHERE THE ROCK HAD BEEN REMOVED. A LITTLE LATER, THE CATACOMBS WERE ALSO DUG BENEATH THE CITY. AS THE CITY EXPANDED, THIS CREATED A PROBLEM. THE CITY'S **FOUNDATIONS** ARE WEAK. IN 2011, 44 STRUCTURES COLLAPSED. IN 2013, ANOTHER 83 STRUCTURES COLLAPSED. URGENT WORK IS TAKING PLACE TO REBUILD THE CITY'S FOUNDATIONS TO STOP MORE BUILDINGS FROM COLLAPSING!

VIETATO L'INGRESSO

This abandoned house is closed but to visitors because it is in danger of collapsing at any time.

17

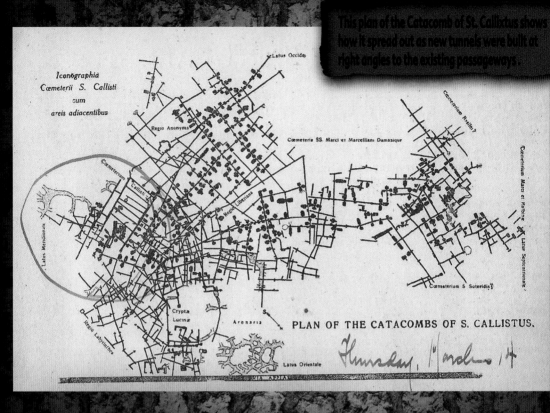

Iconographia
Cœmeterii S. Callisti
cum
areis adiacentibus

PLAN OF THE CATACOMBS OF S. CALLISTUS.

Among the oldest and largest of the Christian catacombs are the Catacombs of Domitilla. They are named for Saint Domitilla. She was a granddaughter of the Emperor Vespasian who likely converted to Christianity.

The galleries were probably excavated between the late 100s and early 200s AD. Their galleries stretch over 10.5 miles (17 km). Around 150,000 people were buried there. The Catacombs of Domitilla are decorated with Christian paintings, including the fish symbol used by early Christians. They also have an underground **basilica**, or space for religious services.

HOW RICH ARE YOU?

LIKE ANY CITY, THE CATACOMBS HAD EXPENSIVE AND CHEAPER AREAS. PEOPLE WERE BURIED DEPENDING ON HOW MUCH MONEY THEIR FAMILY COULD PAY. THE BEST SITES WERE CLOSEST TO THE TOMB OF A SAINT. SOME WEALTHY FAMILIES WERE BURIED TOGETHER IN THEIR OWN SIDE ROOM. THE POOREST PEOPLE COULD NOT EVEN AFFORD FUNERAL NICHES. THEIR CORPSES WERE PILED UP ONE ON TOP OF ANOTHER. WHERE SPACE WAS TIGHT, SOME BODIES WERE LEFT IN THE GALLERIES.

This stone marked the tomb of a woman named Licinia Amias. The fish were a Christian symbol, because Jesus was described as a "fisher of men."

When the catacombs were first built, they were used for burials. Later, they took on another function. Some catacombs contain larger underground rooms. These rooms may have been used for religious services.

For many years, experts believed that these rooms were used for Christian worship. They knew that Christians were persecuted in Rome in the 300s AD. They guessed that the catacombs had been used as secret places of Christian worship.

A PLACE OF WORSHIP?

Experts now know this conclusion was mistaken. Christians did worship in the catacombs, but only much later, after Christianity became the state religion of the Roman Empire in AD 380. After 380, the catacombs became the destination for Christian **pilgrims**. It was then that the mythology grew, suggesting the tombs had been a hiding place for early Christians escaping Roman persecution.

Some catacombs contained larger spaces that experts once thought were used for secret worship.

From the 300s AD more people visited the catacombs. Church services were held there. Many visitors came to see the tombs of **martyrs** who had died for their faith. Many believe that Nereus and Achilleus were killed because of their beliefs during the reign of the Emperor Diocletian. Their tombs were visited by pilgrims for centuries.

WHAT DID HAPPEN UNDERGROUND?

Some underground rooms in the catacombs have benches lining the walls. Experts think visitors would have used the benches when they came to eat with their dead relatives. They think early Christians held picnics with the dead, similar to what some Mexicans do on the Day of the Dead. In Mexico, the Day of the Dead is a holiday honoring dead relatives. Many families visit the graves of their loved ones and bring food, flowers, and candles.

KILLED FOR THEIR RELIGION

THE EARLY EXPLORERS OF THE CATACOMBS BELIEVED THAT THE TOMBS HELD THE BODIES OF CHRISTIANS WHO HAD DIED FOR THEIR BELIEFS. BEFORE THE EMPEROR CONSTANTINE CONVERTED TO CHRISTIANITY IN 312, CHRISTIANITY WAS ILLEGAL IN ROME. THOUSANDS OF ITS FOLLOWERS WERE KILLED BY THE ROMANS, BUT MANY HUNDREDS OF THOUSANDS OF PEOPLE WERE BURIED IN THE CATACOMBS. THEY WERE NOT ALL VICTIMS OF PERSECUTION.

Christians pray in the Colosseum, where they are about to be killed by lions in this 19th-century painting.

Of the more than 100 miles (160 km) of passages in the catacombs, many have not been fully explored. Until the early 2000s, archaeologists did not have the tools to study individual catacombs in detail, but advances in technology changed that situation. In 2006, a joint team of Italian and Austrian scientists, architects, and archaeologists began to study the Saint Domitilla Catacombs in detail.

The catacombs stretch for miles over four stories. Today, however, only a third of a mile (500 m) is accessible to the public. The archaeology team used a 3D laser to scan the whole catacomb in order to make a **digital** model of its structure and its decorations. The experts placed a scanner in hundreds of different locations in the catacomb.

EATING WITH THE DEAD

THE PRACTICE OF SHARING A MEAL WITH DEAD RELATIVES DID NOT ONLY EXIST AMONG THE ROMANS. IN MEXICO, FOR EXAMPLE, THE PRACTICE DATES BACK MANY CENTURIES. IN THE PAST, MANY PEOPLE BELIEVED THAT THE DEAD RETURNED TO EARTH ON ONE DAY EACH YEAR. WHEN THEY CAME, THE DEAD NEEDED FOOD AND DRINK. EVERY YEAR ON NOVEMBER 2, MANY MEXICANS STILL VISIT THE GRAVES OF THEIR LOVED ONES TO BRING THEM FOOD AND DRINK.

25

This arched chamber in the Catacomb of St. Callixtus was used for the bodies of early popes.

The 3D laser scanner used by the team at the Saint Domitilla Catacombs sent out millions of light pulses. These bounced back off of every surface they hit. The scanner recorded these pulses as billions of white dots. As the scientists gradually moved the scanner along the passages, these white dots were put together to build up a 3D picture of what each space looked like. The dots created a 360-degree moving model that could be studied on computers.

The scanner revealed wall paintings that have not been seen for centuries. Because they had been in the darkness underground, they had not faded from the effects of sunlight. The colors were perfectly preserved. The paintings were still as bright as when they were first created.

One mystery of the catacombs is just who was buried there. Experts know that early Christians, Jews, and others were buried there. They also know that some specific Christian martyrs and early popes were probably buried there. But today the identities of most of the dead have been lost. Some tombs are still marked with the name of a family, but most inscriptions are gone. Most bones and coffins are gone, leaving empty spaces.

Some experts suggest that as many as six million people were buried underground. At one time, historians believed they were all Christian martyrs. Today, scientists know that there were not that many martyrs. But we will probably never know the identity of more than a few of the people who were buried in the catacombs 2,000 years ago.

This statue from the Saint Domitilla Catacomb shows the Good Shepherd, a character from a Bible story.

THE PAST

For about 150 years from the early 300s, Rome was attacked by a series of peoples the Romans called "barbarians." Experts think these invaders probably robbed the catacombs when they attacked Rome. This might explain why so little has been found inside the tombs. From the 500s, the catacombs were abandoned. The entrances became overgrown. As Rome expanded, all visible signs of the underground world beneath its streets disappeared.

The last emperors of Rome are thought by many to have been weak. They allowed the empire to collapse around them.

MONVMENTVM PRIMVM ARCVATVM COEMETERII
SS·HERMETIS BASILLÆ PROTHI IACINTHI
VIA SALARIA
VETERI

A CHANCE DISCOVERY

On May 31, 1578, workers found a stairway on Via Salaria to the north of Rome. It was the entrance to the Catacomb of Priscilla. The discovery attracted great interest, but no one really understood its importance. Fifteen years later, however, an enthusiastic young archaeologist began to investigate.

Antonio Bosio had decided at age 18 to dedicate his life to archaeology. In December 1593, he began to explore the catacombs. He guessed that the catacombs were connected to the early Christians. He began to study early Christian texts, looking for information about the passageways.

THE FALL OF ROME

IN THE 300s AND 400s, THE ROMAN EMPIRE IN THE WEST WAS THREATENED BY GERMANIC PEOPLES ON ITS EASTERN BORDERS. THE EMPIRE WAS SIMPLY TOO LARGE TO DEFEND, AND A SERIES OF WEAK AND SHORT-LIVED EMPERORS WERE UNABLE TO PREVENT ROME'S DECLINE. THE "BARBARIAN" PEOPLES GAINED IN STRENGTH UNTIL, IN 476, THE EMPEROR ROMULUS WAS OVERTHROWN BY A GERMANIC LEADER NAMED ODOACER. THE ROMAN EMPIRE WAS AT AN END.

Romulus (left), the last emperor of Rome, hands power to the Germanic leader Odoacer in 476.

The entrance to the Catacomb of St. Callixtus was hidden beneath this entrance arch.

Antonio Bosio questioned local people about any other forgotten entrances to the catacombs. Using the information, Bosio eventually found 30 more entrances. It was not easy. During one 18-year period, he found only two entrances.

These were the very early days of archaeology. Bosio did not record everything he found. Some of his conclusions about the catacombs were inaccurate. Still, his hard work was a good starting point for later archaeologists.

FAST FORWARD

Investigation of the catacombs halted for 200 years until Giovanni Battista de Rossi began his studies in the 1840s. De Rossi was a pioneer of what is known as Christian archaeology.

In 1849, de Rossi rediscovered the Catacomb of St. Callixtus on the Appian Way. When excavation began in 1852, evidence showed that nine third-century popes were buried there. Fifteen years later, de Rossi published *La Roma Sotterranea Cristiana*. The book described the tombs as places of Christian burial and worship.

MORE DISCOVERIES

After Giovanni Battista de Rossi's work, archaeologists continued to work underground. In the 1900s more catacombs were discovered, in 1956 and again in 1959.

SARCOPHAGVS MARMOREVS: EX VATICANO
COEMETERIO EFFOSSVS

This drawing was made by Antonio
Bosio. It shows carved icons he had
found in the catacombs.

ROMA SOTTERRENEA

IN 1632, BOSIO'S WORK *ROMA SOTTERRANEA* WAS PUBLISHED AFTER THE
AUTHOR'S DEATH. THE BOOK WAS THE CULMINATION OF BOSIO'S MANY YEARS
OF STUDY AND EXPLORATION OF THE CATACOMBS. BOSIO DESCRIBED ALL THE
CATACOMBS HE HAD EXPLORED, BEGINNING WITH THE CEMETERY AT THE VATICAN
AND FOLLOWING A COUNTERCLOCKWISE DIRECTION AROUND ROME. THE BOOK
INCLUDED MANY OF BOSIO'S OWN DRAWINGS OF THE CATACOMBS. IT WAS THE
FIRST TIME MOST PEOPLE HAD EVER SEEN WHAT THEY LOOKED LIKE.

In addition to the new catacombs, a different type of underground structure had also been uncovered. In 1917, workers were digging a new railroad on the outskirts of Rome when a tunnel collapsed. It revealed an entrance to a hidden place of worship, now called the Basilica of Porta Maggiore.

A PAGAN PLACE OF WORSHIP

The chamber was older than the Christian catacombs. Experts believe it was built in the first century AD by a wealthy Roman family. The family is thought to have belonged to a minor **cult** based on the writings of the Greek philosophers Pythagoras and Plato.

The basilica was dug out of the soft tufa 40 feet (12 m) below the ground. Archaeologists working there revealed **reliefs** that included images of gods, goddesses, panthers, and winged cherubs, or angelic beings. The basilica even had an arched ceiling. Now about 2,000 years old, the chamber has been renovated and is open to the public.

The arched ceiling of the Basilica de Porta Maggiore was discovered early in the 1900s. It was built and decorated about 2,000 years ago. It was sealed up during the reign of Emperor Claudius in the 40s and 50s AD.

PAST VS. PRESENT

THE MODERN CITY OF ROME IS JUST THE LATEST OF MANY CITIES TO HAVE BEEN BUILT IN THE SAME SITE ON THE TIBER RIVER. THIS MAKES IT DIFFICULT TO MODERNIZE THE CITY. FOR YEARS, ROMANS HAVE WANTED A BETTER AND BIGGER SUBWAY SYSTEM. EVERY TIME WORK BEGINS TO EXPAND THE SUBWAY, IT HAS TO STOP WHEN NEW ARCHAEOLOGICAL REMAINS ARE FOUND DEEP UNDERGROUND. ROME'S RICH HISTORY IS STOPPING THE DEVELOPMENT OF THE MODERN CITY.

How can the subway in Rome be expanded when engineers keep discovering ancient ruins?

TODAY

As Roman streets collapse, more ancient secrets are revealed. In 2002, a burst water main caused a tunnel to collapse. Experts who were called in found a medieval **fresco**. They believe it shows two Christian saints, Peter and Marcellinus. The saints appeared to be guarding a group of burial chambers. They are called the "X" tombs, because on Vatican maps the site was marked with an "X.""

THE "X" TOMBS

Archaeologists found hundreds of bodies packed tightly together in six underground rooms.

There are reminders all over the city of the ancient network of drains and

Were they Christian martyrs, or victims of some **plague**? Experts used **DNA** testing, **radiocarbon dating**, and even a new method of testing the DNA in teeth to find the answers. Analysis of the bodies was still going on a decade after they were discovered.

The first thing the experts learned was that the bodies would have filled a larger space than the rooms they were buried in. That revealed that the bodies must have been buried at different times. The earliest burials had decomposed before later burials were added.

The skeletal remains showed no signs of violence. The people were probably not Christian martyrs. Experts did discover, however, that none of the people seemed to have been very old when they died. In which case, what had killed them?

One answer may be linked to Rome itself. Rome was the biggest city in the world in the early centuries AD—but it was also filthy. The Romans enjoyed visits to the public baths, but experts now believe the baths helped to spread diseases. Dying from disease was a common occurence in ancient Rome.

These ruins of a public bathhouse are in Leptis Magna in Libya. Did Roman baths help spread disease?

The teeth of the dead can reveal information about a person's life that is not detectable from other bones.

TESTING TEETH

THE INVESTIGATION INTO THE "X" TOMBS HAS INVOLVED CUTTING-EDGE TECHNIQUES. AMONG THE MOST EXCITING NEW METHODS IS THE ANALYSIS OF TEETH FROM THE SKELETONS. A PERSON'S TEETH REVEAL INFORMATION ABOUT THEIR YOUTH. BONES CHANGE DURING OUR LIVES, BUT SCIENTISTS LEARNED THAT THE MINERALS IN TEETH ARE SET FOR LIFE IN CHILDREN. WHEN ANALYZING TEETH FROM THE "X" TOMBS, SCIENTISTS NOTICED THAT ONE MINERAL THAT WAS COMMON IN ROME, OXYGEN-18, WAS MISSING. THAT LED THEM TO BELIEVE THAT THE PEOPLE HAD NOT ORIGINALLY COME FROM ROME.

Experts used radiocarbon dating on organic remains from the linen shrouds and pieces of thread found in the "X" tombs. They discovered that the bodies in the two larger chambers were buried in the 100s and 200s AD. The bodies in the other three smaller chambers dated from the first century AD.

DNA traces in the teeth of the skeletons suggest that the bodies in the larger chambers were most likely killed by the Antonine plague. This was a serious disease known to have struck Rome between AD 165 and 180 and again in AD 189.

In this mural from the wall of a catacomb, St. Peter heals a sick woman who touches his robes.

Experts believe that at least 2,000 bodies were buried in the tombs. Tests on the skeletons, fabric, and soil in the tomb showed that the dead people were well fed and had come from all over the Roman Empire. As victims of various outbreaks of the Antonine plague, they had been piled together rather than being buried individually.

Experts now believe the bodies might have belonged to members or family members of the emperor's elite **cavalry** division. If too many of the cavalry had died at the same time all from the plague, there would not have been room to bury them in cemeteries. The cemeteries would have been full.

The ruins of the Colosseum and Forum of ancient Rome are surrounded by a crowded, busy, modern city.

DISCOVERY AND PRESERVATION

FOR ARCHAEOLOGISTS IN ROME, THE DISCOVERY OF NEW FINDS SUCH AS THE "X" TOMBS IS BOTH EXCITING AND CHALLENGING. THEY LEARN MORE ABOUT ANCIENT ROME NEARLY EVERY DAY. THEY HAVE TO WORK WITHIN A BUSY MODERN CITY, HOWEVER, SO THEY NEED TO BALANCE THEIR WORK WITH THE NEED FOR NEW CONSTRUCTION IN ROME. IN ADDITION, THERE IS GREAT PUBLIC INTEREST IN NEW DISCOVERIES, SO EXPERTS HAVE TO FIGURE OUT HOW TO DO THEIR WORK WHILE ALLOWING PEOPLE TO ACCESS ANY NEW SITES THEY DISCOVER.

MORE TO LEARN

The discovery of the "X" Tombs shows that there is still much to learn about the catacombs. Not only may more discoveries come to light. Advances in science also allow experts to gather much more information from older finds. They can correct mistaken assumptions made in the past—but they can also open whole new areas of investigation that will fill out more information about the hidden catacombs beneath the city.

What secrets still remain to be discovered among the miles of buried passageways beneath Rome?

TIMELINE

Ancient Romans begin burying rather than cremating the dead.

Death of Jesus. His death inspires the rise of the Christian religion.

Construction begins on the Catacombs of Domitilla in Rome.

A serious outbreak of Antonine plague hits Rome.

Another outbreak of Antonine plague occurs in Rome.

Emperor Diocletian launches his Great Persecution, during which thousands of Christians are killed for their faith.

Emperor Constantine converts to Christianity after seeing a sign in the sky during the Battle of Milvian Bridge.

The Edict of Milan makes Christianity legal in the Roman Empire.

Christianity becomes the official religion of the Roman Empire.

Emperor Romulus is deposed by a Germanic chief named Odoacer, bringing an end to the Western Roman Empire.

May 31: The Catacomb of Priscilla is discovered. It is the first catacomb known to modern Romans.

Antonio Bosio begins an archaeological examination of the Catacomb of Priscilla during which he also discovers more catacombs.

Published after his death, Bosio's book *Roma Sotteranea* summarizes his discoveries and contains drawings of the catacombs.

Catacombs are built in Paris, France, when the city's graveyards become full.

Italian archaeologist Giovanni Battista de Rossi rediscovers the Catacomb of St. Callixtus.

De Rossi publishes *La Roma Sotteranea Cristiana* ("Christian Underground Rome").

While digging a railroad, workers find an underground Christian church, the Basilica of Porta Maggiore.

A small catacomb is discovered in Rome. It seems to have been a private catacomb for a few wealthy families.

More catacombs are discovered in Rome.

A burst water main leads to the discovery of burial chambers known as the "X" Tombs for the way they were marked with a cross on Vatican maps.

The Domitilla Project uses 3D scanning technology to examine the Domitilla Catacomb, enabling experts to re-create its early decoration.

apostles The disciples of Jesus.

archaeologists People who study history by examining old structures and artifacts.

basilica A large public building or church.

catacombs Underground cemeteries formed of passageways with niches for bodies.

cavalry Soldiers who fight on horseback.

converted Changed from one religion to another.

cremated Burned into ashes.

cult Religious devotion to a person or object.

diaspora The dispersion of Jews from the Holy Land.

digital Created and stored on computer.

DNA Deoxyribonucleic acid, the material by which parents pass on genetic information to their children.

excavated Uncovered in a methodical way.

foundations The lowest parts of a building or city.

fresco A painting done straight onto wet plaster.

funerary Relating to a funeral or the commemoration of the dead.

inscriptions Words carved into a hard surface, such as stone.

martyrs People who are killed for their religious or other beliefs.

milestones Stones that indicated each mile along a Roman road.

niches Shallow areas or shelves hollowed out of a wall.

pagans People who hold religious beliefs different from the main religions of the world.

persecuted Treated badly or killed because of one's race or political or religious beliefs.

pilgrims People who travel to a sacred place for religious reasons.

plague A highly contagious disease that is often fatal.

radiocarbon dating A method of telling how old objects are by measuring their carbon content.

reliefs Carvings that stand out from a wall.

sarcophagi (sing. sarcophagus) Stone coffins.

volcanic Describes rock created by the eruption of a volcano.

Books

Coddington, Andrew.
Martyrdom: Christians in the Roman Empire (Public Persecutions). New York: Cavendish Square Publishing, 2017.

Dickmann, Nancy.
Ancient Rome (History Hunters). North Mankato, MN: Capstone Press, 2016.

Holtzer, Ben.
Religion in the Roman Empire. (Life in the Roman Empire). New York: Cavendish Square Publishing, 2017.

Von Finn, Denny.
Paris Catacombs (Scariest Places on Earth). Minneapolis, MN: Bellwether Media, 2013.

Websites

www.catacombe.roma.it/en/catacombe.php
The official page of the Roman Catacombs in English, with links to articles about their history.

http://www.pbslearningmedia.org/resource/nvrc-sci-whoxtombs/whos-buried-in-the-x-tombs/
A short video from PBS about the scientific analysis of the bodies found in the "X" Tombs.

http://science.nationalgeographic.com/science/archaeology/rome-catacombs/
An article about the mysteries of Rome's ancient catacombs.